In memory of Karen

(October 27, 1955—October 8, 1976)

table of contents

...

preface

"**Who** is Dorothy Childers—and what right does she have to tell me that I *can* and *should* prepare for grief and proceed to tell me how I can go about doing it?"

I don't profess to be an expert. I've experienced grief and I've given a lot of thought to the reaction to loss. I've come to some conclusions which I've been sharing with others as I've spoken to church and community groups since 1986. These are opinions—either my opinions or the opinions of experts I agree with. (These experts are acknowledged in the list of references.) My intent is not to get you to agree with me; it is to get you to do some creative thinking with your families, come to your own conclusions, and make your own decisions.

our daughter died

When our 20-year-old daughter Karen was killed in a single-vehicle accident in 1976, a number of friends told my husband and me that the way we handled our grief was an inspiration to them, and they urged me to write about it. As I began analyzing our personal experience with grief, I realized that much of our ability to cope had been conditioned ahead of time.

not completely
unprepared to grieve

It's assumed that whenever we experience grief, we are never fully prepared to cope with it. However, we are not totally *unprepared* to cope with grief, either. We turn to whatever resources we have to pull us through—and we can begin to develop more of those resources now.

more to grief than
tragedy and pain

Many authors of books about grief deal with sorrow while it is experienced, but writers rarely infer that there are some things you can do ahead of time. Psychologists write about the necessity to grieve, implying that it will probably be a lengthy sorrowful period, full of tragedy and pain. Psychiatrists discuss diagnosis and treatment of pathological grief and depression, but not prevention. Movie reviewers ridicule sentimental movies which show a character dying without inconvenience or bitterness and the survivor grieving with dignity. Dictionaries use only negative terms in their definitions of grief: intense, painful, regret, suffering, and woe. I suggest that there are other characteristics of normal, healthy grief. Coping with grief can have positive attributes, too, but you have to be ready for it.

prepare for old age

Advice for preparation for old age is available in the categories of physical health and finance. A number of people over 100 years old were interviewed on the television program, "20/20." It was observed that they had one thing in common (and it was neither *wealth* nor *good health*): they were all able to cope with grief. They appeared to be coping graciously with being old.

a hope to cling to

I suggest there are ways in which you can help yourself and your family be better prepared to grieve. I hope you'll share this book with your family. Keep the ideas that you think are helpful, talk about the things you disagree with, and develop your own theories. It won't keep you from grieving—in fact, it is important that you *do* grieve—but it may help you through the stages of sorrow as you react to a loss, and the suggestion that you *will* get through the ordeal may give you the hope that, someday, you'll need to cling to!

the final event of life

Since Karen's death, I have lost my parents and my parents-in-law. All four of them were elderly and in deteriorating health—the opposite situation of the sudden death of our first-born child, a healthy, happy 20-year-old young woman. Each of those five deaths was the final event in their lives—final, important events—and I believe that the family coped with their deaths in such a way that we enriched our own lives and added dignity and honor to each of those who died.

why read this now?

It will be easier for you to read this at a time when a mourning situation is merely a hypothetical one. If you are actually experiencing one of the stages of grief, thinking about it may be painful, and something that I consider a sensible suggestion could sound to you like a smug, "pat" answer—one that you aren't in the mood to consider. But if you're not grieving at this moment and are able to store up some ideas, you'll be able to draw on them when you need them and know that they'll be helpful.

Because it is something I have experienced, I frequently refer to things you can do ahead of time to prepare your family in case one of your children dies. They say that is the worst grief; so if you can consider ways to handle the worst, it should help you handle anything.

an explanation

Throughout this book I refer to my family (husband Tom; children Karen, Laurie, Amy, and Joel; sister Georganne) and friends by name. Occasionally, when identifying people might embarrass them, I have changed their names.

My religious background as a Christian Protestant (United Methodist) strongly influences my opinions and the words I use to describe them. Having a common language does not guarantee that we always understand each other. Those of us who use similar words to describe our beliefs often mean entirely different things and some of us who share similar opinions often use different terminology to describe those ideas. I do not visualize God as the stately gentleman with a long white beard I imagined Him to be when I was a child. Now I acknowledge that the image of God is beyond my comprehension, but I still call God "He." If my referring to God as "He" disturbs your image of a deity, or if I don't include beliefs that are important to your faith, I hope you'll make the appropriate substitutions so that this book will be useful to you.

. . .

1...
admitting that it can happen to you

We may not want to think about it right now, but there are many times during each of our lives when we grieve. There are many "lesser" griefs as well as "overwhelming" griefs.

We will grieve whenever we are disappointed, when things don't work out the way we want them to; we will grieve each time we experience a blow to our dream of an ideal life, which includes a "perfect" marriage and "perfect" children but doesn't include disappointment or sorrow.

We will grieve over the loss of anything important to us: if we lose our job, retire, lose our sight or our hearing; when we are angry at a friend or a spouse; when we have to move away from friends; and when friends move away from us.

We will grieve if our child is unhappy or injured or handicapped, if we learn he is promiscuous or on drugs or gay; and we will grieve if we experience the "empty nest syndrome."

We will grieve if we go through a divorce, if we have to move into a nursing home or find it necessary to put a parent into one, or if we suffer the death of a loved one or a friend; and we will grieve when we are facing our own eventual death.

Grief is the difficult but necessary process of dealing with any loss. No one is exempt. No matter what causes our grief, it feels like a gigantic wound that cannot be mended.

that won't happen

It is instinctive to react to the first hint of impending death with, "That won't happen!" We don't want it to happen; therefore, we don't believe it can happen. When we're told that a loved one has died, our immediate response is, "No!" We live in a society that has avoided or ignored the subject of death. We feel uncomfortable talking about death, and we prefer to be comfortable.

it could happen
to any of us

If we admit, now, when we're not thinking about a specific person, that it could happen, that someone we love could die at any time, then, when the time comes that we must accept that a loved one is terminally ill or has died, the adjustment will perhaps be more gentle.

Accidents, illnesses, violence, severe weather conditions—any number of things—could cause the death of one—or all—of our children, within the next year, or month, or minute. As they are growing up, we do what we can to protect their health and safety, but obviously we can't have as much control over their circumstances as we'd like. We can pray for their protection, and I feel certain that doing so will increase their protection as well as help our peace of mind, but we know that someone's child is dying right now, and someone else's child is going to die in a few minutes. It happens, and it can happen to us.

• • •

2 ...
deciding how your faith will help you

You need to feel comfortable about your own religious beliefs. There are some, especially those who have yet to experience tragedy in their family, who don't find conflict in the idea that good people often suffer even though God is all-powerful and is also just and fair. I have a Presbyterian friend whose belief in predestination helps her accept anything as "God's Master Plan," and that is obviously a belief she is comfortable with. My Christian Scientist father-in-law didn't acknowledge anything that was not good, and that worked for him. I know others who find comfort in blaming Satan for all grief situations, and that certainly gets God "off the hook" for them.

But not everyone is as confident in his or her religious theories as the people in these examples. I have seen Christian friends feel guilty as they struggle with a grief they think they shouldn't show and an anger they can't help feeling towards God. I think it *is* hard to love a God who decides to have good people suffer, who decides to permit a hurricane to kill hundreds of people, or who decides that it is His will that your—or my—child die.

nurturing spiritual life

It is very helpful to develop a belief structure that includes some understanding of God's will before disaster befalls us. When the worst happens to us, it is probably too late to formulate a deep faith if it isn't already developed.

Find the Bible verses and other writings—now—which could give you the most comfort and which confirm your beliefs. You'll want to be able to refer readily to them when you need to.

Even though I don't mean to infer that you should believe the same way I do, especially if your beliefs work for you, I will explain how I feel about God's involvement since it was crucial in my family's grief-healing.

God's will: His "hope" for what we do with our lives

Romans 8:28 is often quoted to the bereaved: "And we know that all things work together for good to them that love God." If I interpret this as "things that happen are God's will and are a part of God's good plan," then that verse will only remind me of my anger toward God. (And grieving people *do* feel anger!)

Not long before Karen's death, our church women's group in Mandeville, Louisiana, studied Leslie D. Weatherhead's book, *The Will of God.* From that study, I came to believe that God created for us a universe that had to include certain rules. Since He decreed these rules, He isn't going to interfere occasionally with the laws of nature (like gravity) and mathematical laws (like the law of chance) in order to prevent death.

In fact, if everything that happens can be considered as "God's will," then why should we pray that God's will be done? Can't God make sure His will is done all by Himself? I believe that God's "will" is God's "hope" or "wish" for what we will do with our lives. I believe it is God's will that we work together with everything that happens in our lives in order that good might come from each experience; that we come through each tragedy that befalls us, as well as the good times, with good relationships with God and with those around us. People are never the same after experiencing grief, and so they will either grow closer or grow apart. Surely it is God's will that we grow closer, that we listen to each other and comfort each other.

everything that happens isn't God's intention

When Karen died, a sympathetic neighbor came to see me, delivering a plate of brownies and the statement, "We know it is God's will." Paula's husband had died of cancer, and she had met and fallen in love with and married a man whose wife had committed suicide. Paula's face beamed as she declared that the perfect example of God's will was the wonderful family she and Jim and the combination of their six children made. Now, I can't believe that a loving God would sacrifice Paula's first husband and Jim's first wife because He preferred to have the eight of them as a family!

"Accidents do happen, but I'll be there to help you."

I said, "I'm certain that if I had asked God the morning of October 8 if He wanted Karen to die, His response would have been, 'No, I rejoice in her exuberant life, but accidents do happen and I don't control those things. The girl driving the truck this afternoon may drive too fast, or the truck's mechanism may be faulty, or the road may need repair. I don't want her to die, but if she does, My will is that you cope with your grief, and I'll be there to help you!'"

don't get stuck on anger

It was very helpful for us *not* to blame God for Karen's death—or to blame anyone else. Resentment hinders the healing process during grief. It was even suggested that we sue her employer, the Forestry Department. What would that have done other than prolong our grief and delay our healing? Expressed anger creates a whirlpool; we get stuck there and can't move beyond it.

When a friend's husband told her that he wanted out of their 29-year-old marriage because he had a young girlfriend, Mary was understandably shocked and hurt but she has reacted with love and concern for her husband and has urged her family and friends to think kindly of him. It's amazing what her attitude has done for herself and for all of us. Her positive attitude has enabled her to get on with her life— quite quickly, in fact.

the promise of peace

"Peace I leave with you" (John 14:27) is a promise from God. It doesn't mean that we will be surrounded by peaceful situations; it means that no matter what situations we are in, if we believe in Him, we will have peace. I have found that with God's help we are able to respond to *life* with *love* and, by doing so, we find that promise of *peace*. Nothing can happen to us that is more than we can handle if we turn to Him. (But we can make it easier to handle if we have done some preparation ahead of time.)

God was with us, too!

A well-meaning friend wrote to us after Karen's death, "I know what you are going through. Our daughter was in a serious accident two years ago and almost died, but God was with us, and she lived." Well, let me tell you, God was with us, too! God *is* with us. He is sympathetic and supportive and will guide and comfort us as well as sustain us. His presence and His promise of peace are there for the asking.

. . .

3 ...
talking with your family: concepts and decisions

Once you have developed some positive theories about your faith and how it will help you in times of sorrow, I hope you will want to share your ideas with the rest of your family.

include the children

We adults tend to shield our children from the grim realities of life—especially death. We think that if we don't talk about problems or crises, they will just go away.

Children are exposed to death from time to time, either when their pet or someone they know dies or when they see someone die on television (in fiction or on the news), and they may be confused and upset. Awareness of the loss of a life should be dealt with immediately. Parents need to know just exactly what is on the child's mind; sometimes the fantasy about a situation is worse than the reality.

Death is part of our lives, and acknowledging it is part of growing up. If we can help our children cope with events they're exposed to as children, it will help them handle these issues as adults. It will be easier to talk to children about this subject before something terrifies them.

I like my minister's description of the baby leaving his comfortable world and "dying to the womb" as he is born into a world beyond his comprehension. And so will we, one day, "die to this world" into a world beyond our comprehension. This concept might appeal to children. Delores Kuenning devotes a chapter on "How to Talk to Children About Death" in her book, *Helping People Through Grief,* which you will find helpful.

Talk with your family about what they think happens to people before and after death. Elisabeth Kübler-Ross' book, *On Death and Dying,* is very comforting and would be a good springboard for such a discussion. Her interviews with terminally ill patients support the Bible's promise of life after death and provide courage to those who are approaching death. If we believe in life after death, then death is a brief separation.

get your affairs in order

There are some very practical decisions that families can and should make ahead of time: legal updated wills, detailing who should raise the children if the parents die prematurely; the many-faceted, sensitive subject of home care and nursing homes; whether or not to fill out "living wills" and "durable power of attorney for health care;" the type and place of burial; the funeral service; and maybe even the obituary.

Add as many things to this list as you can. In other words, get your affairs in order and keep them in order. Pay your debts, or make arrangements to do so. Itemize your "treasures" with their estimated value and any other information you know about them. Either give them away to your heirs or designate who should inherit them unless you prefer that they be sold as part of your estate after you die. Let someone, especially the one you have named executor of your estate, know where your important papers are and include as much information as you can with those papers. Consider all the things someone might need to know after you die. My husband, as executor of his father's estate, arranged to sell his father's home. The realtor needed to know where the septic tank was and how deep the well was, and my husband didn't know.

At the time of death, the survivors have to make a lot of arrangements while they are under stress. They want to "please" the loved one who died, but also need to make plans that will give themselves comfort. If all members of a family know ahead of time how the others feel about these decisions and discuss their differences, then the decision-makers will know what plans to make.

personal belongings

Tell your family what you want done with your personal keepsakes after you're gone. Karen had saved every letter she had ever received. We didn't know whether to throw them away or return them or read them or just keep the box. Years later, that box is still among our belongings. Decisions are easier if you talk about them when you are still talking about hypothetical situations.

I kept a few other things of Karen's that I didn't want to throw away: some dried wild flowers she'd been collecting in Idaho (I had a pine cone wreath made, incorporating her collection, and it is hanging above our fireplace) and her favorite dress (eventually I cut the fabric to make a quilt square for our granddaughter).

the funeral and legal instructions

When my father died in 1982, my mother arranged for his funeral, and she also planned her own: who was to sing, what she wanted him to sing, whom she did *not* want to play the organ, and what she wanted included in her obituary. My sister ordered the music and had everything ready. When Mother died on New Year's Eve, 1988, we knew what to do. Following her wishes gave us great pleasure in the midst of our sorrow.

A "living will" usually requests that if "I" should have an incurable injury, disease, or illness, "I" direct that life-sustaining procedures be withheld or withdrawn and that "I" be permitted to die naturally with only the administration of medication or the performance of a medical procedure deemed necessary to provide me with comfort, care, or relief from pain. You are probably aware that once a mechanical means of prolonging life (and often that just means prolonging dying) is initiated, it is nearly impossible to reverse the decision—to "pull the plug." As long as both of my parents were alive, one of them was there to make health care decisions about the other. After my father died, my sister and I had that responsibility for our mother. Mother had us promise "not to let them put tubes down her throat again." There was no "plug to pull." Mother was given medication for pain, but no tubes. Her breathing shortened and she died peacefully.

type of burial

The summer before Karen died, my mother was treated for a recurrence of cancer, and she talked to me about anticipating her own death. I was surprised when she told me that she wanted to be cremated, and that initiated my thinking and reading about cremation. An article in *Reader's Digest* described it as "a glorious brilliant light" as opposed to "slow decay," and I thought "that sounds great for Mother!" When we suddenly had to make decisions about Karen's body, we were one step ahead in deciding what to do.

many decisions

Tom and I had many decisions to make when Karen died—all while we were in a state of shock. Someone had to accompany Karen's body as it was brought home to Louisiana from Idaho, and we thought perhaps we should make that painful trip. (Karen was majoring in forestry at Louisiana State University and worked for the U. S. Forestry Department each summer.) Johnny, Karen's friend who was working for the Forestry Department with her, flew home with her body and stayed until after the memorial service. We were fortunate to be able to stay at home during the initial shock of grief. My heart goes out to those who have to grieve in public, especially in front of a TV camera.

In order to stimulate your own family's discussion, I'll tell you some of the other decisions we made:

- deciding between a funeral or memorial service
- selecting the location of the service
- specifying the wording of the obituary
- planning the service
- disposing of the ashes

We went to the funeral home to make arrangements and ended up disagreeing with the funeral director about almost everything. Two dear friends— our very assertive, supportive minister and an equally assertive, supportive neighbor—went with us, and they both urged Tom and me to make our own decisions and insist on them.

The funeral director wanted services at the funeral home; we wanted a memorial service, but not at the funeral home. He agreed to have it at our church. At that time our new Methodist church was meeting in a warehouse; so we said that we'd like to have the service at Fairview State Park, a riverside park nearby that our family had enjoyed together. A private memorial service out-of-doors on public property had never been requested in St. Tammany Parish, we were told, but the park officials were very cooperative and we treasure the appropriateness of the location of that service.

The director at the funeral home balked initially at our request that friends plant trees somewhere instead of sending flowers. Trees were planted in

Karen's memory, we were told, all over the world—
in England, Israel, and across the United States.

therapeutic assertiveness

Personnel at funeral homes and hospitals can,
unintentionally, be very intimidating to the bereaved
family. The uniqueness of our arrangements gave us
a boost and, I'm sure, speeded up our healing. Being assertive during the appointment at the funeral
home and laughing about it later was wonderful
therapy.

A woman told me, after attending one of my
programs, that when she priced caskets for her
husband's body, she asked the director of the funeral
home if they gave senior citizen discounts. Very sol-
emnly he told her, "We couldn't. Most of our cus-
tomers *are* senior citizens!" She and her daughters
still giggle about that.

the appropriate service

Because he knew us so well, our minister's suggestions for the memorial service were very appropriate, and it was a meaningful service for the family and the friends who attended. My mother's new
minister barely knew the elderly woman who was
no longer active in her church. After Mother's death,
my sister and I reminded the minister that our

mother had been the organist at that church many years ago. To our dismay, he built his whole funeral sermon around Mother's musical contribution to life! There was so much more to her than that! The Quaker faith has a meaningful memorial service with everyone sharing his memories of the one who died. Be sure to arrange for an appropriate service for your loved one, as well as for yourself. You won't get a second chance!

the final details

One of our hardest decisions concerned the disposal of Karen's ashes. We didn't want to bury her ashes in New Orleans and have a tombstone in a cemetery we would someday be moving away from. Eventually, the next summer, we went on a family camping trip on the East Coast, and we spread her ashes in the Smoky Mountains. The 10-month delay to pick up the canister of ashes was a nagging unfinished business for us as well as a nuisance for the folks at the funeral home. We wished we had done something sooner, but we have no regrets about returning her ashes to the earth and in one of the places she'd been and loved.

Let your family explore together the funeral or memorial service of your tradition. Consider the memories your family cherish and somehow weave them into the service. Be creative. Helpful booklets are available. Ask your ministers and look for them in your church library or at book stores. Any decisions you make together, as a family, will be appreciated later by those who are mourning, and they will be more meaningful because you made them together.

• • •

4...
getting involved in other people's grief

A week after our daughter died, a widow in her late thirties, whom I barely knew, said to me very bluntly, "Well, have you gotten used to it yet?" It took me a moment to realize that she was actually referring to our daughter's death. I don't remember what my stunned response was. I was upset by her question, and it wasn't until much later that I realized that perhaps she *had* "gotten used to" her husband's death, and sharing some of her experiences would have helped me in my grief—if she had chosen a tactful approach. (Perhaps she hadn't adjusted to his death, and that explains her tactlessness.)

how to express concern

Before we can express concern, we have to feel a genuine concern for people. I find that, as I pray for someone, my compassion becomes stronger. In fact, it is virtually impossible for me to *avoid* expressing concern when I care about someone.

Getting involved in other people's grief involves visiting those who are terminally ill as well as expressing concern to those who are grieving. The advice given for one will apply to the other.

what to say

It's not up to you to give the "right" answer to pleas of "Why me?" and "I know I'm not getting better." In fact, familiar clichés can do more harm than good. Consider how harmful the following "words of comfort" might be:

- "Things could be worse."
- "God is testing you."
- "You're young; you can have another baby."
- "It was God's will."
- "It's all for the best."

emotional support

1. **Be there.** You may be reluctant to visit the friend who is seriously ill or is grieving over something other than her own illness because it's difficult to watch a friend suffer. You may be tempted to avoid the experience by staying away entirely—or perhaps you go, but ignore the reason you're there. Go! Don't miss the opportunity to help your friend and deepen your own spiritual life.

2. **Use the power of touch.** Hold her hand, pat her on the arm, hug her. If your friend is grieving or is lonely or fearful of the future, your touch will mean a great deal.

3. **Listen.** The friend who is in the midst of a divorce may need to tell you the details again and again. The friend whose child died may want to reminisce.

4. **Don't feel you need to give the "right answer" to a statement or question.** Saying "I can see you're really troubled by this" is a more helpful response than "God is testing you." Parents of a five-month-old baby spent several days and nights in a hospital, waiting for the diagnosis of their baby's illness. When they knew how serious it was, they were still unable to leave. A nurse in the intensive care unit comforted them with the words, "I can't make him well, but I can love him." Those words released them from their vigil. They could go home, knowing there was someone there who would love him.

5. **Validate the person's emotions.** Rather than responding, "Don't talk that way," if the patient says to you, "I know I'm not getting better," reflect what they're feeling so that they know you understand. You might say, "I'm sorry that you're feeling very discouraged and scared about your condition." Actually, if a member of the family is dying, towards

the end, she may be wanting to hear a release from you, waiting for your permission for her to die.

6. **Don't be afraid of tears**—the patient's or your own. Saying "Don't cry" is more hurtful than it is helpful because bottling up emotions is unhealthy. Tears help heal grief.

7. **Understand the five stages of death and dying:** denial and isolation, anger, bargaining, depression, and acceptance. This can help you identify and accept your friend's feelings of the moment.

8. **Remember that hearing is the last sense to go.** Don't talk about him as though he weren't there. You can speak or sing to a dying person and he will be probably be aware.

9. **Keep each visit brief.** Remember to follow up with other visits, phone calls, notes, and cards as often as you can.

10. **Be yourself.** It is reassuring during such visits to find that the grieving person is still the friend you know and love, and your friend will be reassured that you are still yourself.

practical support

In addition to emotional support, there are some practical ways to help someone who is grieving:

- Help with everyday chores.
- Assist with cards and letters.
- Lend a hand with meals.
- Buy her a massage.
- Offer childcare.
- Invite her to dinner.

When you are visiting someone who is dying or someone who is grieving, try to place yourself in that position and consider what would be most helpful to you. It will help you as you console others and will help you know what will console you when you grieve.

words of consolation

"When you are sorrowful—
Look again into your heart,
and you shall see
that in truth
you are weeping
for that which has been your delight.
May delightful memories fill your
sorrowful heart with joy."

A friend shared with me this sympathetic sentiment that you may occasionally find to be appropriate. (Perhaps, originally, this was a message on a printed card. If you write it in a personal sympathy letter, it may be more meaningful.)

what not to say, when not to say it

Within these pages, I mention situations that did not ease my grief, and I refer to some things that people said or did that were very helpful. I also talk about ideas I stored away, long before I was in a grieving situation, that were very helpful to me.

If I am told, under normal circumstances, that God does not give me more that I can bear, then later, when I am grieving, it may comfort me to remember that I will be able to endure my grief.

But if a "sympathizer" makes a similar remark while I am grieving, I may think she is unsympathetic. "Test" your sympathy letter for "insensitivity." Put yourself in the receiver's place—would the letter you're writing comfort you?

We should be aware of our shortcomings and acknowledge that humans aren't perfect. The one asking, "Why me?" is probably thinking, "Why not you?" and the comforter, as she is saying, "I'm so sorry," is also thinking, "I'm glad it's not me." We shouldn't be ashamed of this normal reaction, but tact and common sense prevent our expressing all of our feelings and compassion helps us forgive the griever if she expresses hers.

acknowledge sorrow

I don't know if everyone who is grieving craves to hear from friends as much as I did. That Christmas I wrote everyone we send Christmas cards to and told them about Karen's death. We sent a picture of the five of us taken a few weeks after her death—a happy picture. We wanted to share our sorrow with our friends and let them know that we were going to "make it."

We eagerly waited to receive a letter from each of them, and we cherished each response. Some never did write. Like many of us, they probably didn't know what to say, but when I got ready to write notes on Christmas cards the next year, if we had not heard from them since I wrote the year before, I couldn't think of a thing to write to them; so I just signed our names. (Some of these "old friends," when we saw each other years later, said right away, "I wanted to write when I heard that Karen had died, but I didn't know what to say.")

Any time you don't know how to respond to a friend's grief, remember that it will be appreciated if you send a card and add a note saying, "I wish I could express myself, but I am too upset and don't know what to say." No matter how painful or difficult it may be, it is important for you to be supportive to your friends by acknowledging their sorrow and your own.

One friend sent me several magazine articles she had saved (some of which I've used as reference material) with a brief note saying, "These articles may be of help to you. I've been thinking of you for the past two days. What a loss and sadness must fill you." It was a simple message, greatly appreciated.

Another friend wrote to us three or four times, about a month apart. It meant so much to us, knowing that she was continuing to think about Karen and about us.

hand-written messages

I almost always hand-write sympathy letters even if I use the convenience of my word processor to compose them because I think that even a few hand-written words on a card are read and appreciated much more than the printed words on the card.

Even when I don't personally know the person who died, I can write to my friend:

The thought that always gives me peace when I am grieving for someone dear to me is the reminder that I am grateful for her life and for my part in her life and hers in mine. And though we always wish we had them with us longer, we can thank God we had them with us as long as we did.

And I sometimes add that we realize that the separation is but for a short time.

Whenever I write notes of sympathy, I try to say something positive:

(if the death was sudden) *I know you're grateful that he didn't suffer.*

(if the death occurred after a long illness) *I know you are grateful that you were able to be with her.*

Feelings of gratitude are good feelings. They can make anyone feel better.

. . .

5...
strengthening relationships

Because Karen left us in May to work in the forests in Idaho for six months, we had said a lot of "good-bye's" and "I love you's." Letters and phone calls were frequent and loving.

Younger sister Laurie visited Karen that summer and we were all grateful that Karen and Laurie had that time together.

a good relationship

At the time Karen died, we all felt pretty good about our relationship with her. I can't stress strongly enough just how important that was to us.

She loved her work, she loved us, she knew we loved her, she was "on top of the world." She was on her way to fight her first forest fire (!) and that made it easier to "give her up." Regrets, especially our own omissions or mistakes toward the relationship, surely hinder the healing process.

something to do— now

One thing you can do now and never regret doing is to strengthen relationships and, if necessary, repair those relationships—not only with your family, but with *all* people you care about.

the risk is worthwhile

There is a risk here, of course: the closer you are to someone and the more you love someone, the deeper your grief will be if you are separated. But the risk is worth it. Not only will you have fewer regret should she die and be able to experience normal grief, but you will be developing a support group to sustain you when you are grieving. In fact, write or telephone all those old friends you've been intending to write and haven't. Forgive all the people you've been holding a grudge against and tell them so. Apologize to all those you've offended.

Get in the habit of living in such a way that you say "I love you" to the people you care about while they can still hear it. If I should die today after I'd told my family that I loved them, then at least they'd know I cared about them. Or if today I heard that a loved one had died, at least I'd be consoled by the knowledge that he knew I loved him. And, if there had been a strain in our relationship in the past—if

there had been something that should have been for-
given and forgotten—I'd want to be able to add:
"Thank heavens that was no longer an issue in our
relationship!"

. . .

6...
thinking positively

Practice replacing thoughts of regret with positive thoughts of gratitude. It *can* be done. It's hard to think of two things at the same time so force another thought to take the place of the thought that is too painful to dwell on. It takes some practice, but whenever my mind was imagining the truck Karen was riding in, turning over..., I forced myself to think of something else. The thought that was most comforting to me was the realization that at the time of Karen's birth we had been willing to take the risk of loving and raising a child when there was no guarantee that she would live even 20 years and how grateful we were for those 20 (almost 21) years. The idea came from a poem sent to us by a young friend, a poem written by Edgar Guest after a schoolhouse in Texas exploded, killing a number of children.

no guarantee

A dialog is initiated by God in the poem, "To All Parents." God says that He will lend a husband

and wife one of His children for them to love while she's alive and mourn for when she dies. There's no guarantee as to how long the parents will have her —it may be just a few years, it may be until she's an adult. God says that He specifically selected these parents to teach the child the lessons He wanted her to learn. He asks them if they're willing to give birth to this baby and love her for whatever length of time they have her and not feel that it was all in vain if the time came, prematurely, for her to return to Him.

The parents reply that of course they're willing to take the risk of grief. They look forward to the joy the child will bring to their lives and they will remember, in the midst of their grief, how grateful they were for the opportunity.

willing to take the risk

I realized when I read the poem (and I read it over and over again) that this really was the "bargain" we all make before we become parents. We want a baby! It's not that we want a baby who's going to live until she's 87 years old! We hope she'll outlive us, we expect her to outlive us, but no matter how short her life is, we want her anyway. What a difference that concept made in the quality of my grief!

express gratitude
for life

Being able to express gratitude for the life of a loved one who dies is wonderful therapy. In most circumstances, there are things you might regret, but there are always things you can find to be grateful for. Look for them. Hopefully, you should find them within your religious faith.

The Christian concept of life-after-death and the belief that, when we also die, we will join them again is a comforting reassurance. Those who believe in reincarnation find comfort there. Others feel that through meditation and prayer they are able to have access to the spirit of the person.

why not me?

The griever who asks, "Why me?" might just as well ask, "Why *not* me?" Why was Karen killed in an accident? All of my children have been involved in accidents or near-accidents that might have killed them. Shouldn't I ask, "Why me, *only* this one time? Why *not* me, *four* times?" It certainly reminds me that I have a great deal to be grateful for.

coping with stress

Grief is one of the causes of stress in our lives, but we have some control over how we react to stress and we can improve our ability to cope before the stress exists. Grief *can* bring out feelings of compassion for others who have experienced grief. This is a more positive response than the devastating feeling that you're the only one who has endured what you are going through.

Becoming old and dependent upon others is another stressful situation we face with great reluctance. Characteristics such as pride and self-centeredness will make our final years even more stressful. We need to get into the habit of being a "good sport" so that we will become "sweet old ladies (or men)" rather than "old grouches" whom no one wants to be around!

We can't expect to get our own way (or have a tantrum when we don't) every time something less serious than a death in the family occurs, and then expect to cope with the severe grief that faces us if our child dies. "Spoiled brats" don't handle crises well at all!

our children are lent to us

In his book, *The Prophet*, Kahlil Gibran reminds us (as did Edgar Guest's poem) that our children are not "our" children, that they come through us but do not belong to us.

The mother of the child who goes off to college can cope with the "empty nest syndrome" if she has enjoyed interests and activities not connected with her family life. She can begin letting go of her children emotionally years before they go off on their own. The realization that our children are in our care for only a few years and that they will leave home one day should be in our thoughts years before it happens. In this way, we will not burden them or ourselves with sadness when the time of departure arrives.

This is not to say that if her child dies, the mother won't experience great sadness, but if she was prepared to cope with something she knew was going to happen—the inevitable departure of her child from the home, then she would be better prepared, if necessary, to cope with the untimely death of the child.

practice being a good sport

I've had a few bouts of bad sportsmanship in my lifetime and have finally decided to save the tantrums for those devastating occasions over which I might possibly have some control. There don't seem to be very many of those; so I've become a pretty good sport, and that attitude comes in handy.

A test of good sportsmanship occurs for me every time a good friend moves away or I move away from friends. Writing letters to folks we miss is a lot better than not ever having had them as good friends. I remind myself that if everyone I miss were living in my community, I wouldn't have time to be a good friend to all of them—and, since that's not an option anyway, I'll just do the next best thing! We write to each other, comfort each other, phone occasionally, and even visit each other whenever possible.

If you're a good sport, you'll set a good example for those around you—your children, your friends, your spouse. We know that the mother who is afraid of cats will pass on that fear to the young child who sees her reaction to a cat. Surely the parent who is hysterical when the child's grandparent dies passes that reaction to grief on to her child. Talk about the loss and show emotions (both sorrow for the loss and joy for having known them), and you'll help your child do the same. If you don't talk about the death with him, a deception will exist between the two of you and this could lead to problems.

some thoughts to remember

"Act enthusiastic and you'll be enthusiastic" is a Dale Carnegie motto, and it works most of the time. The bottleneck is in *wanting* to be enthusiastic.

Again, I think we get help here through our Christian faith. We are able to "live as if we know tomorrow will be better than today, even though common sense gives you odds that tomorrow will be the pits!"

Faith is an expression of positive thinking. Through our Christian faith, we can believe the Bible verse, Psalms 118:24: "This is the day that the Lord has made; let us rejoice and be glad in it."

. . .

7...
considering the concept: our loved ones are always a part of our family

I have heard of people whose grief is so unbearable that they put away all reminders of the one who died, even refuse to let anyone mention his name. What a shame!

What we love about someone is the life and spirit he expresses, rather than the "material package." When he is gone, that spirit remains, and our loved ones are always a part of our family. This is true whether they live near us or not and *whether they are alive or not!*

We easily accept the concept that distance doesn't keep our loved ones from being a part of our family. Members of our family may live many miles from us, but we enjoy hearing what they're doing and looking at pictures of them and we look forward to seeing them. They're in our thoughts and are certainly a part of our family.

When we read a letter from a friend, the expression of caring about us is as valid as it was several days earlier when the friend wrote the letter and will continue to be each time we read the letter.

when the passage of time separates us

When our daughter Amy was three years old, she was darling! She said such cute things and was a joy to be around. Three-year-old Amy isn't here any more, but we still enjoy remembering the funny things she said.

when death separates us

Karen isn't here any more either, but our memories of the 20 years of her life are as much a part of our family as our memories of three-year-old Amy.

they're still an influence

My mother has been a steady influence on me. During the last 30 years of her life, we weren't together very often, but she affected my cooking, my decorating, my shopping, my attitude toward life. I was aware then that when she died, she would still affect my cooking, my decorating, my shopping, my attitude toward life. And she does.

fond memories

Before my father's death in 1982, Tom and I often referred to a corny joke as a "George Brown joke" or commented on how much Daddy would appreciate a lovely piece of furniture or carved wood, and we continue to do so. Daddy always enjoyed reading the *Reader's Digest*, and he constantly read things out loud to us, even if we were reading something else. Whenever I start to share something with Tom that I'm reading in *Reader's Digest*, I chuckle as I think of my father. Daddy gave Tom a woodworking tool that he especially liked, and Tom thinks of him whenever he uses it. How wonderful it is to be able to continue enjoying someone we love even after he has died!

Karen is still a part of our family with all of her faults as well as her wonderful qualities. She was everyone's best friend in the family, a real peacemaker, and we often talked about how she would have handled some friction between the sisters and brother. Karen never did take good care of her clothes, and as her sisters and I one day were sorting through her things that were sent home to us, we fussed about a stain or a rip that she hadn't mended. We were relieved as we realized that we were criticizing her instead of putting her on a pedestal. The *whole* memory of her is definitely still a part of our family.

love doesn't die

Love doesn't die; the physical body does. Tom's mother had Alzheimer's disease. We began grieving about 10 years before her death, but we didn't love her any less. Our memories of Frances as she used to be, as well as our good-natured recognition and acceptance of her disoriented state, kept her a very active participant in the family during those final years, and now, after her death, she is still very much a part of our family.

bittersweet thoughts

So, Karen, the 20-year-old—as well as Karen, the 5-year-old, and Karen, the 10-year-old—is still a part of our family. The Karen that *isn't* a part of our family, the Karen that will never be, is the Karen who died when she was almost 21, who would have matured as her sisters and brother have, who perhaps would have married and had children, who would have met a sister for lunch or sympathized with her brother when he lost his bicycle or sent me a Mother's Day card and a birthday gift.

Thinking about this is "bittersweet," and I do indulge myself *occasionally*, but dwelling on it is painful. That's when I have to think of something else. Maybe Karen's life, if she had lived, wouldn't have been happy. Maybe, maybe... Who knows? I *am* grateful for the 20 years of her life. I *am grateful!*

• • •

8...

knowing what to expect during grief

There are some very good books you should borrow and read—ahead of time. Buy the ones that are the most helpful, and keep them in your home. One of my favorites is Granger E. Westberg's *Good Grief.* As the author describes the feelings you are experiencing as you grieve, you realize that you are not the only one who has felt as you are feeling. And you know what is coming next. It is normal, it is universal, and it is healing. As you heal, it gets easier.

Another book I enthusiastically recommend is Norman Vincent Peale's *The Healing of Sorrow.* His three pages on accidental death are wonderful. Joyce Landorf's *Mourning Song* reinforces the belief that *without* God's positive reinforcement of love, death becomes a long tunnel ending with a brick wall instead of a bright opening to a glorious new life.

The book, *How to Survive the Loss of a Love,* by Melba Colgrove, Harold H. Bloomfield, & Peter McWilliams, has many practical suggestions of things to do that will comfort and help. It was written in 1976, but I wasn't aware of it until someone recommended it to me in 1990. I wish we had known about it in 1976. A friend recommends the workbook by the same authors called *Surviving, Healing & Growing* that helped her adjust to a divorce.

initial response

The initial response to grief is a blessing: when sorrow or pain is overwhelming, the griever is in shock, is temporarily anesthetized. Dr. Kübler-Ross recommends not sedating the grieving family. She says that if they can experience the pain and anguish and express it, their grief is much shorter afterward. Otherwise, they go through it all in a mechanical, numb kind of dream state, and the truth hits them at the worst time—when they're sitting alone. She recommends volunteers who have experienced similar griefs "staff" a room for bereaved families at the hospital, near the emergency room, and even follow up weeks later to see if the family would like to talk to the volunteer. Dr. Kübler-Ross is exceptional in that she recognizes the value of non-professionals.

know how others react

It would be beneficial if members of your family were aware of how each other reacts under stress.

Dr. Harriet Goldhor Lerner, psychologist and author of the books, *The Dance of Anger, The Dance of
Intimacy,* and *The Dance of Deception,* describes in
the *Intimacy* book circumstances that lead a couple
to divorce. When their six-year-old daughter was
physically disabled in a car accident, the mother's
reaction to her grief was depression; the father's was
distance. Perhaps, if we're aware of how differently
we respond under stress, we will be able to be more
tolerant of each other. Divorce is not an uncom-
mon consequence of parents' incompatible grieving.

Parental reaction to the disclosure of homosexu-
ality, if the parents disapprove of that lifestyle for
their child, can result in alienation from the son or
daughter, and even divorce, if the parents cannot
ride together through the stages of grief I imagine
they must experience. The organization P-FLAG
(Parents and Friends of Lesbians and Gays) has many
members who are survivors of grief, able to choose
to love and support rather than alienate.

the stages of grief

Westberg describes in his book, *Good Grief,* the
stages a griever may go through:

- in a state of shock
- expresses emotion
- feels depressed and very lonely

- may experience physical symptoms of distress
- may become panicky
- may feel a sense of guilt about the loss
- filled with anger and resentment
- resists returning to normal activities
- gradually hope comes through
- struggles to affirm reality

This list is very similar to Dr. Kübler-Ross' stages of grief the terminally ill go through (denial and isolation, anger, bargaining, depression, acceptance). It is useful to consider the stages the griever may go through as long as we remember that they do not always occur and, when they do, they are not always in this order or of equal duration nor need they be devastating.

If you have grieved—*because* you have grieved—you can probably identify with many of the experiences listed above. You can improve the quality of each of these expressions of grief if you can remember to think of others. Perhaps the following story will be as helpful to you as it was to my family.

thinking of others

Twelve years before Karen's death, the 15-year-old son of our good friends was accidentally shot to death by his best friend who was showing off his father's rifle. Within hours after their own son's death,

Anne and Morgan were at the hospital to comfort the young friend who was in shock and to comfort his parents. That impressed us so much—to think that they would be able to think of someone other than themselves at a time like that!

We may never know when something's going to make an impression on us or how it will affect our responses years later. We found that we were able to be concerned for the woman who was driving the truck Karen was riding in, and we phoned her in the hospital to see how she was and to let her know we cared about her, that we didn't blame her. We wouldn't have been able to do that—it would never have occurred to us—if not for Morgan and Anne. And that helped our healing process.

others are hurting besides you

That brings me to another point I hope you'll remember: other people are hurting besides you. That is hard to realize because during the early stages of grief, you are the center of your world—the only one you're aware of who's hurting. And that's just not true. Our family grieved, as a family, but each member of the family also grieved separately. (Sibling grief is especially severe and often overlooked by those comforting the parents.) My husband's family and my family grieved because they loved Karen, but they also grieved for us and it was very hard for them. Karen's friends were grieving for themselves, the girl who drove the truck must have been grieving, the people Karen worked for and with were grieving, her teachers at Louisiana State University were grieving. Everyone whose life had been touched by Karen was suffering. People we didn't know, would never know about, were grieving.

the worst grief of all?

I said at the beginning that grieving about the death of your child is considered the worst grief of all. I'm not sure that is true. Widowhood is probably lonelier. A heart-breaking divorce is a blow to your self-esteem. Grief about the alienation of a child from your family would be full of regrets. Of course, in some of these situations, there's the hope that things will change. Death is permanent, but the mother grieving the death of her child gets overwhelming love and support and sympathy. The mother whose daughter has messed up her life, or the wife whose husband has left her, may not get that same response from others. Friends are wonderfully patient and supportive when your child dies.

• • •

9...
knowing what to do about it

Knowing what you might expect to experience when you are grieving is helpful. So, too, is knowing how to live with loss. Don't just let grief happen to you! There *are* some things you can do about it!

physical needs

There are practical suggestions for meeting your physical needs during grief:

- Get plenty of rest.
- Be alert to stress-related health problems.
- Keep yourself healthy.
- Do some vigorous exercise for mental and physical well-being.
- Take pride in your physical appearance.

emotional needs

The 10 chapters of this book form a list which recommends things to do *ahead of time* to *prepare* for grief. The following list describes things you can try to do *while* you are grieving to meet your emotional needs (and you will know you will be able to do them because you will be prepared):

1. Accept the reality of death. Karen's friend, Johnny, was the one who phoned us and told us she had died. I imagine it would be very hard to believe a message like that if you didn't know the person who called. Johnny was crying; we had to believe him. And *believing* is the first step in the healing process of grief.

2. Accept your feelings. Express your feelings aloud even when it makes you cry—*especially* if it helps you cry. Don't try to avoid crying. When I'd wake up at night, during the months after Karen's death, thinking about something that made me sad, I was tempted *not* to share it with Tom, to spare him that particular sorrow, but if I kept the thought to myself, I would be lonely and perhaps be resentful that my husband was able to sleep peacefully while I was so miserable. By sharing thoughts with him and his sharing similar moments with me, we managed to get a lot of hurdles out of the way. Doing it together made it easier.

3. Draw upon your faith for consolation. Read the books and Bible verses or other sources of inspiration again and again—things you will have already selected and set aside, things that you know will help you. Think about things that appealed to you as you were preparing yourself for grief. Remember how grateful you are for the life of the loved one and concentrate on how brief the separation will be.

4. Keep your loved one a part of your family by talking about her. Remember the funny things, the good times, even the "less-than-perfect" things about her. Help your friends feel comfortable. Let them know you appreciate talking about her.

5. Appreciate your relationships with other people. Think of others. Be aware that other people are also grieving. Express your appreciation for your relationship with them. Participate in the present as much as possible. Try to be "fun" to be with whenever possible.

6. Let people know what you need. Let them know when you want to be alone and when you want company. Ask for and accept help. (The practical suggestions of how to help others, mentioned in Chapter 4, are things your friends will be willing and eager to do for you.) Express your appreciation of their attention. Get medical diagnosis and help if you suspect your grief is not progressing normally. Be aware that, despite great sadness, hope should still be present.

7. Be patient with yourself as you adjust. Don't feel guilty when you're not feeling sad. Certainly the person you loved would want you to heal and be happy with life.

Be kind to yourself, even pamper yourself.

Try to relax and keep a sense of humor whenever it is possible. I mentioned how refreshing it was for us to laugh about the meeting with the funeral director. There was another comical moment we remember:

One evening, several weeks after Karen's death, our 10-year-old son, Joel, made instant chocolate pudding for the family for dessert. Instant pudding may have improved in recent years, but it was pretty awful that night. Rather than hurt Joel's feelings by saying we didn't like it, each of us said, "Joel, I'm not very hungry; you can eat my pudding." Just then the phone rang, and as our daughter Amy answered it, she said, "It must be another order for Joel's chocolate pudding!" Amy couldn't talk because she was laughing so hard, and so she handed the phone to me, and I was laughing, too, and couldn't talk. The friend on the phone thought we were crying, and she felt terrible. It was hard for her to believe our family could find anything to laugh about. At times it was hard for *us* to realize that we had so much fun at the dinner table that evening, but remembering that we had gave us hope that we would again.

8. Then strive to regain a positive outlook by setting goals and working to reach them and by trying new activities. Make the decision that you want to have a happy, interesting future. Plan to telephone a friend each day, or write a letter, or start keeping a diary, or get your hair done, or do something artistic or creative. Set simple goals at first. Gradually you will be able to expand your social life and resume your volunteer work and/or your career, or perhaps enroll in a class at your local community college. Try to reach out and expand your activities at a pace that challenges you and keeps you busy but doesn't create stress. Your friends will help you.

9. Remember, no matter how bad it gets, it will get better!

For many years I got very flustered when I answered the question, "How many children do you have?" (I've been told of a man who tells people he has three sons: one who lives in Colorado, one who lives in Texas, and one who lives in Heaven.) I used to write the return address on Christmas cards and letters from the family, "Childers 6." I never wrote, "Childers 5."

Setting the table for five for Christmas dinner in 1976 was very painful. Sometimes it still is, even now—just a twinge—still, it's there, but it gets easier. *It gets easier.*

I dreaded those first holidays; in fact, I felt worse the day *before* each of them, I dreaded them so. Setting the table for five instead of six was always terrible that first year.

I thought that first year was sad! The next Thanksgiving, a year later, Tom was watching football on TV and the kids were all doing something, not helping me, and I had to set the table (for five) by myself and no one was feeling sorry *for* me or *with* me!

Enjoy the warmth of shared grief. It gets better (but sometimes it gets lonely before it gets better!).

Don't forget, if ever you are grieving and think you'll never stop, if you think you'll never get any relief from the pain and depression, if you think it won't get better: *it does get easier.*

Taking a picture of the five of us to send with Christmas cards was a great idea! Tom set up his camera with tripod and timer, and then, rather than have only the photographer hurry to get in the picture, we all scattered around the yard and ran to the spot. We had fun doing it, and it showed. *(The picture is on the next page.)*

Knowing that we were able to look so happy a few weeks after Karen's death can be an encouraging reminder to someone who is grieving. We mourned before the moment of the picture, and we certainly mourned frequently after the picture was taken, but there were moments when we actually were happy, and this picture has been a reminder of that.

Remember: no matter how difficult it seems, it *does* get easier. *Much easier.*

This picture of Dorothy, Amy, Tom, Joel, and Laurie Childers was taken several weeks after Karen's death and was sent to friends at Christmas time in 1976. It is a reminder that joy can be present in the midst of grief.

• • •

10...
meeting grief "head-on"

My sister and I were fortunate to be able to spend our mother's last week with her in the hospital as she was dying. Sharing that experience with Mother and Georganne has been a highlight in my life. If I had not been prepared to grieve, I would not have been able to appreciate it!

when it's easier

When the one who dies has led a long, full life, and when our relationship with that loved one is without regrets, and when we have accepted the inevitability that she will die, it is easier to meet grief "head-on" and see to it that our loved one "goes out in style!"

making it special

A friend told me she and her sister sang hymns in the hospital room as their mother was dying. I wish my sister and I had thought of that! Mother would have loved it!

The author Madeleine L'Engle kept a journal as her husband fought a losing battle with cancer. Her book, *Two-Part Invention,* is a tribute to her happy marriage and must have been wonderful therapy for her.

Our friends Bob and Marge lived with Bob's multiple sclerosis for almost 20 years before it finally took his life. They dealt "head-on" with grief every day, courageously, living a good life to the fullest, appreciating their family, their marriage, their friends.

Before my friend Cari died of cancer, she not only planned her funeral, she planned the party to be held after the funeral. Cari always enjoyed giving a party, and I have no doubt she enjoyed planning this one. Her "head-on" strength certainly helped her family and friends share their grief with each other.

A 91-year-old friend of my mother died several years after Mother did. Alice had requested a small funeral service at church—just the family—with an open casket. One of the family members said to the congregation, "If Alice had known how lovely she looks, she would have invited more people to the service!" That humor was a "head-on" tribute to Alice, and certainly lightened the mood of the mourners.

When my daughter Laurie's father-in-law died, his widow included in the notes she wrote to friends who had expressed their sorrow a two-page biography of Alan, compiled by members of his family. They outdid the obituary my sister and I wrote for our mom; I wish we'd have thought of that!

Moving from your family home after 35 years, under any circumstances, would be a time of grief. Charlotte Rosenstock met that grief "head-on" by saying good-bye to her house in a *Reader's Digest* article entitled, "Leaving Home." She told how she and her grown daughters walked through the house, reminiscing, laughing, and crying. They attributed a majesty to their home, and their sustaining memories enabled them to let go and move on. Mrs. Rosenstock lifted up a traumatic event in her life— in the life of her family—and gave it a tribute rather than a lament. Good for her! Don't forget her!

when it's unexpected

We didn't get a chance to say good-bye to Karen. It's easier to meet grief "head-on" if you know it's coming.

But we do know it's coming. There will be a lot of times when we will grieve. Sooner or later, things we hold dear are taken out of our hands. Sometimes gently. Sometimes harshly. But always painfully.

We don't know what the circumstances will be or when they will occur, but we do know that there are things we can be doing, changes we can make within ourselves and encourage others to make within themselves that will prepare us to grieve.

. . .

references and notes

At times when I was grieving, I craved books that comforted me with sentimental thoughts and lulling rhythms. At other times I found strength by reading thought-provoking books offering sensible advice.

The following books and articles are recommended for additional reading. The authors are the experts whose opinions and information helped me sort out my analysis of preparation for grief.

The list includes works that are directly and indirectly mentioned in this book. The page number in this text where a work is directly referenced is shown in the left column.

(frequent Biblical references)

• The Holy Bible, Revised Standard Version (1971), and the New Revised Standard Version of the New Oxford Annotated Bible (1991), Oxford University Press, Inc., New York.

• The Living Bible, paraphrased, Tyndale House Publishers, Wheaton, IL, 1971.

6

• *The Will of God,* Leslie D. Weatherhead, Abingdon Press, Nashville & New York, 1944.

11

• *Helping People through Grief,* Delores Kuenning, Bethany House Publishers, Minneapolis, MN, 1987.

11, 45, & 47

• *On Death and Dying,* Elisabeth Kübler-Ross, MacMillan Publishing Co., Inc., New York, 1969.

12

• "Turning Out the Lights," *Modern Maturity,* June-July 1988 (living will, durable power of attorney for health care).

21-23
- "A thoughtful word, a healing touch," Susan Champlin Taylor, *Modern Maturity*, December '88/ January '89 *(see additional notes)*.

30
- "The Child Will Always Be There. Real Love Doesn't Die," Elisabeth Kübler-Ross, *Psychology Today*, September 1976.

32
- "To All Parents," Edgar Guest (possibly included in *All in a Lifetime*, Edgar A, Guest, Ayer Company Publishers, Salem, NH).

35
- *The Prophet,* Kahlil Gibran, Alfred A. Knopp, Inc., New York, 1923.

36
- *When Bad Things Happen To Good People,* Harold S. Kushner, Avon Books, New York, 1983.

43/46
- *Good Grief,* Granger E. Westberg, Fortress Press, Philadelphia, PA, 1962.

44
- *The Healing of Sorrow,* Norman Vincent Peale, Ballantine, New York, 1952.

44
- *Mourning Song,* Joyce Landorf, Fleming H. Revell Company, Old Tappan, N J, 1974.

44/45
- *How to Survive the Loss of a Love,* Melba Colgrove, Harold H. Bloomfield, Peter McWilliams, Bantam Books, New York, 1976 (and the workbook, *Surviving, Healing & Growing*).

46
- *The Dance of Anger (1985), The Dance of Intimacy (1989),* and *The Dance of Deception (1993),* Harriet Goldhor Lerner, Ph.D., Harper & Row, New York.

52
- "Clinically Significant Differences Between Grief, Pathological Grief, and Depression," John M. Schneider, Ph.D., *Patient Counselling and Health Education,* Fourth Quarter 1980.

58
- *A Two-Part Invention,* Madeleine L'Engle, HarperCollins Publishers, New York, 1988.

59
- "Leaving Home," Charlotte Rosenstock, as quoted by Ron Alexander in the *New York Times, Reader's Digest,* June 1991.

also recommended

• "Losing Someone Close," Dr. Robert DiGiulio, Care Notes, Abbey Press, St. Meinrad, IN, 1988.

• "Finding a Way out of Grief," Annette Jean Hornstein-Janpol, *Christian Science Sentinel,* August 27, 1990.

• *A Boy Thirteen, Reflections on Death,* Jerry A. Irish, The Westminster Press, Philadelphia, PA, 1975.

• "When Someone You Know Is Suffering," Ken Czillinger, Care Notes, Abbey Press, St. Meinrad, IN, 1989.

• "How Can I Live with My Loss?," Tim Jackson, Thomas Nelson, Inc., Publishers, Grand Rapids, MI, 1992.

• *How Can It Be All Right When Everything Is All Wrong?,* Lewis B. Smedes, Harper & Row Publishers, San Francisco, CA, 1982.

• *When You Are Facing Change,* J. Bill Ratcliff, Westminster/John Knox Press, Louisville, KY, 1989.

• *Life Begins at Death,* Leslie D. Weatherhead, Abindon Press, Nashville, TN, 1969.

• "We are Breaking the Silence About Death," Daniel Goleman, *Psychology Today,* September 1976.

• "Coping with Tragedy," an interview with Dr. Janice Hutchinson, *USA Today,* January, 1989.

additional notes

• The ellipsis (…) is a mark indicating an omission of words that, it is assumed, the reader can supply. I use it as a lead into a new chapter and at the end of a chapter. I hope the reader is adding his own thoughts to mine.

5

• I am grateful for the letters, comments, and suggestions from family and friends and for the extensive editing done by my husband, Tom, and my daughter, Laurie Childers (before I gave the manuscript to a professional proof-reader).

• Rabbi Harold S. Kushner, in his book, *When Bad Things Happen to Good People,* says that until he personally experienced tragedy in his family, he had not questioned God's fairness because he assumed God knew more about the world than *he* did. Kushner offers impressive arguments that God does not constantly control things that happen.

5

• Delores Kuenning, in her book, *Helping People Through Grief,* says that it is extremely important to develop a belief structure that includes some understanding of God's will before disaster befalls us.

11

• The Reverend William A. (Buddy) Miller, Kingwood United Methodist Church, Kingwood, TX, used the concept in an Easter sermon to explain the resurrection of Christ. It can be a comforting idea to someone fearful of death.

11

• Delores Kuenning's book, *Helping People Through Grief,* can help you console a friend under almost any circumstance and would be a good study book for a support group to use. Its chapters cover God's will, birth of a handicapped baby, loss of a baby, murder or kidnapping of a child, children with cancer, adoption, abortion, rape, divorce, disfigurement, suicide, catastrophic death, terminal illness, death of a spouse, Alzheimer's disease, nursing home placement, God's promises.

12

• Two places you can write to: A. A. R. P., Widowed Persons Services, 601 E. St. NW, Dept. BL, Washington, DC 20049; and Bereavement & Loss Center of New York, 170 E. 83 St., New York, NY 10028.

14

•A "living will" can also direct that no medication or medical care be given, if that is your wish.

15

• I don't know in which 1976 issue of *Reader's Digest* I read the article about cremation.

19

• Two helpful booklets are: "Planning the Funeral of Someone You Love," Carol Luebering, Care Notes, Abbey Press, St. Meinrad, IN, 1988; and "About Grief," a scriptographic booklet by Channing L. Bete Co., Inc., South Deerfield, MA, 1984.

21-23

• I appreciated Susan Champlin Taylor's article, "A Thoughtful Word, A Healing Touch," on how to make your visit to the seriously ill a positive one and added to her outline. Also, there have been several "Dear Abby" columns responding to tactless comments made by well-meaning friends which let readers realize how offended grievers are at times.

37

• This often-quoted motto is attributed to Dale Carnegie, author of *How to Win Friends and Influence People*, Simon & Schuster, New York, 1936.

38

• Encouragement comes from Lewis B. Smedes in *How Can It Be All Right When Everything Is All Wrong?*, "Grace is a mysterious power to live as if you know tomorrow will be better than today, *even though common sense gives you odds that tomorrow will be the pits.*"

39

• The Navajo practice of not mentioning the one who died is a cultural tradition rather than a reaction to unbearable grief. Living in the present is comforting to them, no doubt. For most of us, this sort of denial may appear to protect us from the anguish of expressing grief, but it postpones healing.

the reader's notes: